Let's Bake

Christmas Treats!

By Ruth Owen

Gareth Stevens
PUBLISHING

Published in 2018 by Gareth Stevens Publishing, 111 East 14th Street, Suite 349, New York, NY 10003

First Edition

Produced for Gareth Stevens Publishing by Ruby Tuesday Books Ltd
Designers: Tammy West and Emma Randall

Photo Credits:
Courtesy of Ruby Tuesday Books and Shutterstock.
Page 4 (bottom) courtesy of Alamy.

Library of Congress Cataloging-in-Publication Data

Names: Owen, Ruth.
Title: Let's bake Christmas treats! / Ruth Owen.
Description: New York : Gareth Stevens Publishing, 2018. | Series: Holiday baking party | Includes index.
Identifiers: LCCN ISBN 9781538213230 (pbk.) | ISBN 9781538213254 (library bound) | ISBN 9781538213247 (6 pack)
Subjects: LCSH: Christmas cooking--Juvenile literature. | Desserts--Juvenile literature.
Classification: LCC TX739.2.C45 O94 2018 | DDC 641.5'686--dc23

Manufactured in the United States of America

CPSIA compliance information: Batch #CW18GS: For further information contact Gareth Stevens, New York, New York at 1-800-542-2595.

Contents

Let's Get Baking!

Falling snow, twinkling lights, decorated trees, and wrapped gifts—Christmas is nearly here. So let's get the party started by baking some delicious, festive treats.

Invite some friends to drop by your kitchen and share in the fun. Let's have a holiday baking party!

Get Ready to Bake

- Before cooking, always wash your hands well with soap and hot water.
- Make sure the kitchen countertop and all your equipment is clean.
- Read the recipe carefully before you start cooking. If you don't understand a step, ask an adult to help you.
- Gather together all the ingredients and equipment you will need. Baking is more fun when you're prepared!

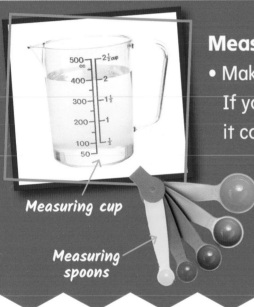

Measuring cup

Measuring spoons

Measuring Counts

- Make sure you measure your ingredients carefully. If you get a measurement wrong, it could affect how successful your baking is.
- Use measuring scales or a measuring cup to measure dry and liquid ingredients.
- Measuring spoons can be used to measure small amounts of ingredients.

Have Fun, Stay Safe!

It's very important to have an adult around whenever you do any of the following tasks in the kitchen:

- Using a mixer, the stovetop burners, or an oven.
- Using sharp utensils, such as knives and vegetable peelers or corers.
- Working with heated pans, pots, or baking sheets. Always use oven mitts when handling heated pans, pots, or baking sheets.

When you've finished baking, ALWAYS clean up the kitchen and put all your equipment away.

Ingredients:

To make the cookie dough:
- 1 ½ cups all-purpose flour (plus a little extra for dusting)
- ½ cup superfine sugar
- 5 ounces butter or margarine (plus a little for greasing)

For the frosting and decorations:
- 1 cup powdered sugar (plus extra for dusting)
- 1 cup water
- Your choice of candy and sprinkles

Equipment:
- 2 large cookie sheets
- Mixing bowl
- Wooden spoon
- Plastic wrap
- Rolling pin
- Set of star-shaped cookie cutters
- Oven mitts
- 2 potholders
- Wire rack for cooling
- Sieve
- Small bowl
- A spoon (for mixing frosting)
- A brush

Cookie Christmas Tree

These **edible** Christmas trees made from star-shaped cookies look great as table decorations. They also make a wonderful homemade holiday gift to give to friends and family members. Have fun decorating the trees with your choice of candies, sprinkles, and glitter, and let your creativity sparkle through!

Step 1 Grease the cookie sheets with a little butter to keep your cookies from sticking to the sheets.

Step 2 Put the butter and sugar into the mixing bowl and **cream together** with the wooden spoon until smooth and fluffy.

Step 3 Add the flour and mix the ingredients with the spoon. Next, use your hands to rub and combine the ingredients until the mixture looks like breadcrumbs.

Finally, use your hands to squeeze and **knead** the mixture to make a ball of soft dough.

Step 4 Wrap the dough in plastic wrap and place in a refrigerator for 30 minutes.

Ball of dough

Step 5 **Preheat** the oven to 350°F (180°C).

Step 6 Dust your countertop with a little flour. Unwrap the dough and place on the dusted surface. Use a rolling pin to roll out the dough to about ¼ inch (6 mm) thick.

Step 7 To make each tree, we cut nine stars in five different sizes from the dough. Place the stars on the cookie sheets.

Step 8 Bake the cookies for about 15 minutes, or until they are turning golden. The centers of the cookies will still be slightly soft, but they'll soon firm up.

Step 9 Remove the cookie sheets from the oven with oven mitts and stand the sheets on the potholders. Allow the cookies to cool for about 10 minutes, and then carefully place each cookie on a wire rack and allow to cool completely.

Frosting

Step 10 For the frosting, use the sieve to sift the powdered sugar into the small bowl. Little by little, add water and mix to make a simple, white frosting. The frosting should be thick, but you must be able to brush it onto the cookies.

step 11 Brush each cookie with a thick layer of frosting.

step 12 To assemble a tree, place a large star cookie on a flat surface. Then carefully stack eight other cookies on top. The cookies should gradually get smaller. Add extra frosting between the cookies as needed to act as glue.

Stand a small cookie on the top of the stack to become the tree's star.

step 13 Once the cookie tree is assembled, you can **drizzle** it with more frosting to look like snow. Alternatively, you can dust the tree with powdered sugar, edible glitter, or other sprinkles.

step 14 Add decorations to your tree such as Smarties or other candies. Use a tiny blob of frosting as glue to hold each candy in place.

Ingredients:

To make the mincemeat:

- Cooking apple
- ½ stick butter
- 1 lemon
- 2 cups each of raisins, golden raisins, and dried cranberries
- 1 cup candied peel
- ½ cup blanched, chopped almonds
- 2 ½ cups brown sugar
- ½ teaspoon pumpkin pie spice
- 1 teaspoon ground cinnamon

To make the pastry:

- 2 cups all-purpose flour (plus a little extra for dusting)
- ¼ teaspoon salt
- 5 ounces butter or margarine
- Water
- Powdered sugar

Equipment:

- Vegetable peeler
- Knife and cutting board
- 2 mixing bowls
- Grater
- Wooden spoon
- Large saucepan
- Rolling pin
- 3-inch (7.5-cm) round cutter
- 2-inch (5-cm) star-shaped cutter
- 2 12-hole pie trays
- Dessert spoon
- Oven mitts
- 2 potholders
- Wire rack

Mini Spicy Christmas Pies

Known as mince pies, these spicy, fruity miniature pies are a **traditional** Christmas treat in Britain. When mince pies were first made hundreds of years ago, they contained minced (or shredded) meat, fruit, and spices. Today, they no longer contain meat, but the fruit filling is still known as mincemeat!

Step 1
Peel the cooking apple and remove the core. Chop the apple into tiny pieces, about the size of peas. Add to the mixing bowl.

Step 2
Cut half a stick of butter into cubes and put into the mixing bowl.

Step 3
Grate the rind of the lemon into the bowl and then squeeze the lemon's juice into the bowl, too.

Step 4
Add all the other mincemeat ingredients into the mixing bowl and stir thoroughly with the wooden spoon.

Golden raisins

Raisins

Dried cranberries

Candied peel

Blanched almonds

Brown sugar

Cinnamon

Pumpkin pie spice

Mincemeat mixture

11

step 5
Scoop the mixture into a large saucepan and place on the stove on a medium heat.

step 6
When the butter has melted, allow the mixture to **simmer** for about 10 minutes, stirring occasionally. Remove from the heat and set to one side.

step 7
Preheat the oven to 400°F (200°C).

Breadcrumb-like mixture

step 8
To make the pastry, put the flour, salt, and butter into a mixing bowl. Using your fingers, **rub in** the butter to the dry ingredients until the mixture looks like breadcrumbs.

step 9
Adding the water a little at a time, gently squeeze and knead the mixture until it becomes a ball of pastry dough. Once you have made a soft dough, stop adding water.

step 10
Dust your work surface with a little flour. Use a rolling pin to roll out the dough to about ¼ inch (6 mm) thick. For each pie, cut a circle to be the pie's base and press it into a pie tray section. Also cut a star for each pie and set to one side. Keep gathering up the spare pastry and re-rolling it to make as many pie bases and stars as possible.

Circular pie base

Spare pastry

Step 11

Put a large spoonful of mincemeat mixture into each pie and top off with a pastry star.

Step 12
Bake the pies for up to 15 minutes, or until the pastry has turned crisp and golden. Remove the pie trays from the oven with oven mitts and stand on potholders. After about 10 minutes, place each pie on a wire rack to cool.

Step 13
Once the pies have cooled, dust with some powdered sugar.

Any spare mincemeat filling can be stored in the refrigerator in an airtight jar for up to one month.

Ingredients:

To make the cookie dough:

- 1 ½ cups all-purpose flour (plus a little extra for dusting)
- ½ cup superfine sugar
- 5 ounces butter or margarine (plus a little for greasing)

For the frosting and decorations:

- 20 large white marshmallows
- Frosting pens
- 1 cup powdered sugar (plus extra for dusting)
- 1 cup water

Equipment:

- 2 large cookie sheets
- Parchment paper (optional)
- Mixing bowl
- Wooden spoon
- Plastic wrap
- Rolling pin
- 3-inch (7.5-cm) round cookie cutter
- Oven mitts
- 2 potholders
- Wire rack for cooling
- Sieve
- Small bowl
- A spoon (for mixing frosting)

Melted Snowmen Cookies

You can make these adorable snowmen-themed cookies to give as Christmas gifts. Alternatively, keep them for yourself and enjoy them on a frosty winter day with a big mug of hot chocolate.

Step 1
Begin by drawing a snowman face on each marshmallow with frosting pens. Allow the faces to set and dry.

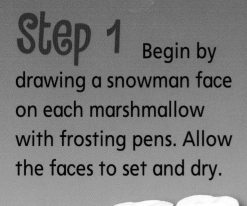

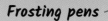
Frosting pens

Step 2
Grease the cookie sheets with a little butter to keep your cookies from sticking to the sheets. Alternatively, lay a sheet of parchment paper onto each cookie sheet.

Cookie sheet

Step 3
Put the butter and sugar into the mixing bowl and cream together with the wooden spoon until smooth and fluffy.

Creamed butter and sugar

Step 4
Add the flour and mix the ingredients with the spoon. Next, use your hands to rub and combine the ingredients until the mixture looks like breadcrumbs.

Finally, use your hands to squeeze and knead the mixture to make a ball of soft dough.

Step 5
Wrap the dough in plastic wrap and place in a refrigerator for 30 minutes.

Step 6
Preheat the oven to 350°F (180°C).

Step 7
Dust your countertop with a little flour. Unwrap the dough and place on the dusted surface. Use a rolling pin to roll out the dough to about ¼ inch (6 mm) thick.

Cut circles from the dough and place on the cookie sheets.

Step 8
Bake the cookies for about 15 minutes, or until they are turning golden. The centers of the cookies will still be slightly soft, but they'll soon firm up.

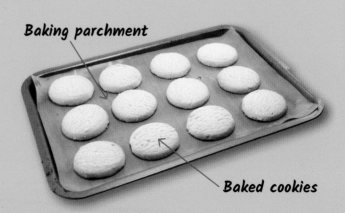

Baking parchment

Baked cookies

Step 9 Remove the cookie sheets from the oven with oven mitts and stand the sheets on the potholders. Allow the cookies to cool for about 10 minutes, and then carefully place each cookie on a wire rack and allow to cool completely.

Step 10 Use the sieve to sift the powdered sugar into the small bowl. Little by little, add water and mix to make a simple, white frosting. The frosting should be a thick liquid.

Step 11 Drizzle a spoonful of frosting onto each cookie to look like a puddle of melted snow.

Step 12 Gently press a marshmallow snowman head into the frosting.

Step 13 Finally, when the frosting has set and is firm, gently draw stick arms and details such as buttons, scarves, or bow ties onto each puddle of frosting.

Serve the cookies with steaming mugs of hot chocolate decorated with more marshmallow snowmen heads.

The quantities on this page will make 1 gingerbread house.

Ingredients:

To make the gingerbread dough:
- 9 ounces butter or margarine
- 1 ½ cups dark muscovado sugar
- 7 tablespoons golden syrup
- 5 cups all-purpose flour
- 2 teaspoons baking soda
- 6 teaspoons ground ginger
- Water

For the frosting and decorations:
- 2 egg whites
- 4 cups powdered sugar
- Water
- Your choice of candies and decorations

Equipment:
- Saucepan
- 2 mixing bowls
- Wooden spoon
- Rolling pin
- Gingerbread house cutters (see step 1)
- 2 large cookie sheets
- Parchment paper
- Oven mitts
- 2 potholders
- Wire racks for cooling
- Sieve
- Electric mixer (optional)
- Frosting gun and teaspoon
- Teacups or small bowls
- Plastic wrap
- A flat wooden board or tray for serving

Gingerbread House

Making and decorating a gingerbread house is the perfect baking activity to do with friends in the days before Christmas. You can buy gingerbread house cutters from baking stores or online. Alternatively, make your own **templates** from clean, thin cardboard. Lay the template pieces on your rolled-out dough and cut around them with a knife.

Gingerbread dough

Cardboard template

1 ½ inches

1 inch

1 ¼ inches

1 ½ inches

1 ¼ inches

Step 1
The ingredients on this page are sufficient to make a house 7 inches by 4 inches (18 x 10 cm) and 7 inches (18 cm) tall.

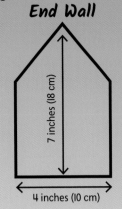

End Wall

7 inches (18 cm)

4 inches (10 cm)

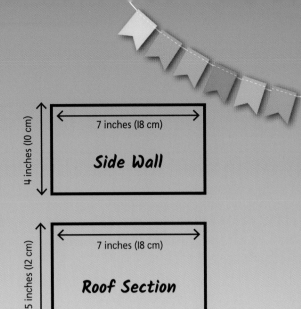

4 inches (10 cm)

7 inches (18 cm)

Side Wall

5 inches (12 cm)

7 inches (18 cm)

Roof Section

Step 2
Preheat the oven to 350°F (180°C).

Step 3
To make the gingerbread dough, put the butter, sugar, and golden syrup into a saucepan. Heat on a medium heat, while stirring with a wooden spoon, until the butter has melted and all the ingredients are combined.

Step 4
Put the flour, baking soda, and ground ginger into a mixing bowl. Pour the butter mixture into the mixing bowl.

Stir the ingredients until they are combined. The mixture will become quite stiff.

Gingerbread mixture

Step 5
Next, use your hands to gently knead the mixture into a ball. If the mixture is too stiff or dry, add a little water.

Ball of gingerbread dough

Cutter

End wall section

Step 6
Place a sheet of parchment paper that's about 10 inches by 10 inches (25 x 25 cm) on your work surface. Break off about one sixth of the dough, place it on the parchment, and roll out until it is about ¼ inch (6 mm) thick.

Cut one piece of the house from the dough.

Step 7
Remove the spare dough. Lift the paper and house section and place on a cookie sheet. Repeat step 6 until you have two roof sections, two end walls, and two side walls.

Any leftover dough can be used to make decorative Christmas trees and gingerbread men.
(Also see the cupcake recipe on page 22.)

Step 8
Bake the gingerbread for about 15 minutes. The edges of the sections should be firm. The centers will be slightly soft, but they'll soon firm up.

Remove the cookie sheets from the oven with oven mitts and stand the sheets on the potholders. Allow the gingerbread to cool for about 10 minutes, and then carefully place each section on a wire rack and allow to cool completely.

Step 9
To make the frosting, put the egg whites into a mixing bowl. Use the sieve to sift 3 ½ cups of powdered sugar into the bowl. Mix the frosting with a spoon or electric mixer until it becomes thick and smooth.

Step 10
Use a teaspoon to fill a frosting gun with the frosting.

Step 11
Begin assembling the house on the wooden board or tray. Glue an end wall to a side wall with a thick strip of frosting.

Use teacups or bowls to keep the pieces upright while the frosting hardens.

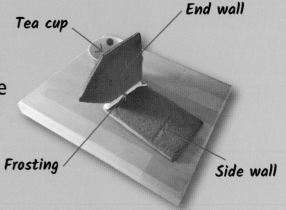

Tea cup
End wall
Frosting
Side wall

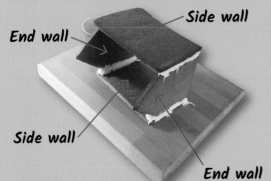

Side wall
End wall
Side wall
End wall

Step 12
Add the second end wall and side wall. Allow the frosting to harden for about an hour. Cover your bowl of frosting with plastic wrap to keep it from hardening.

Step 13
Carefully stand the house the right way up and glue on the two roof sections with frosting. Use any leftover egg white frosting as snow to decorate the house. Leave the house to set overnight.

Step 14
Now the really fun part begins—decorating!

Mix the remaining powdered sugar with a little water to make a thick, glue-like frosting. Stick candies and other decorations to your house with the frosting.

Ingredients:

To make the cupcake batter:
- 7 ounces butter or margarine
- 1 cup superfine sugar
- 2 cups cake flour
- 1 teaspoon baking powder
- ¼ teaspoon salt
- 3 large eggs
- ½ cup milk
- ½ teaspoon vanilla extract

For the decorations and frosting:
- 2 ½ cups powdered sugar
- 1 cup butter
- 4 tablespoons milk
- Green food coloring
- Your choice of green sprinkles
- 12 mini gingerbread men

Equipment:
- 12-hole muffin pan
- 12 muffin cases
- Mixing bowl
- Wooden spoon
- Electric mixer (optional)
- Oven mitt
- Potholder
- Metal skewer
- Small bowl
- Spoon
- Frosting gun

Gingerbread Men Cupcakes

These cute cupcakes are smothered in green frosting and sprinkles, and are topped off with crunchy gingerbread men. You can buy ready-made mini gingerbread cookies or bake your own by following the recipe on pages 18 to 21. If you bake the gingerbread house from pages 18 to 21, you can turn the leftover dough trimmings into gingerbread men decorations for your cupcakes.

Step 1
Preheat the oven to 350°F (180°C).

Step 2
Line the muffin pan with muffin cases.

Muffin pan

Muffin cases

Step 3
Put the butter and sugar into the mixing bowl and cream together with a wooden spoon until fluffy. If you wish, you can use an electric mixer for this step.

Step 4
Add the flour, baking powder, salt, eggs, milk, and vanilla extract to the bowl. Use a wooden spoon or electric mixer to **beat** the ingredients together until the mixture is thick and smooth.

step 5
Spoon the mixture into the muffin cases, dividing it equally.

Cupcake batter

step 6
Bake the cakes for 20 minutes, or until they have risen above the edges of the muffin cases. Using an oven mitt, remove the muffin pan from the oven. To test if the cakes are baked, insert a metal skewer into one cake. If it comes out clean, the cakes are ready.

step 7
Stand the muffin pan on a potholder and allow the cakes to cool completely.

Baked cupcakes

step 8
To make the frosting, mix the powdered sugar, butter, and milk together in the small bowl until thick and smooth.

Step 9
Carefully add drops of green food coloring into the bowl, mixing to get the frosting color you want.

Step 10
Spoon the frosting into a frosting gun with a teaspoon. Gently create a swirled effect on the top of each cake. You can also spoon the frosting onto each cake and swirl with the back of the spoon to cover the top of the cake.

Frosting gun

Step 11
Add green sprinkles to the frosting and stand a mini gingerbread man on top of each cake.

Tie a ribbon or colored string around the gingerbread man's neck.

To decorate the gingerbread men, mix a little powdered sugar with water to create a simple frosting.

The quantities on this page will make one large frosted cake with four layers.

Ingredients:

To make the cake batter:

- 2 cups cake flour
- 2 teaspoons baking powder
- 8 ounces soft, unsalted butter or margarine (plus extra for greasing)
- 1 cup superfine sugar
- 4 large eggs
- 1 tablespoon vanilla extract
- ¼ cup milk
- Red and green food coloring gel

To make the frosting:

- 3 ½ ounces butter
- 8 ½ ounces cream cheese
- 5 cups powdered sugar (sieved)
- White gel coloring for frosting
- Your choice of holiday sprinkles and decorations

Equipment:

- 2 7-inch (18-cm) cake pans
- 2 mixing bowls
- Wooden spoon
- Electric mixer (optional)
- Spoons for mixing
- Rubber spatula
- Oven mitts
- Metal skewer
- Wire racks for cooling
- Sieve
- Medium bowl
- Spoon for mixing frosting
- Serrated knife
- A plate for serving

Christmas Layer Cake

Layer cakes look impressive, but they are actually simple to make—even if you've never baked a cake before. This Christmas layer cake combines layers of red and green sponge cake with heaps of snowy cream cheese frosting. So get ready to impress your friends and family by baking, frosting, and building this fun holiday treat!

Step 1
Grease the two cake pans with a little butter to keep your cakes from sticking. You will be baking the four layers two at a time.

Step 2
Preheat the oven to 350°F (180°C).

Superfine sugar   **Cake flour**   **Vanilla extract**   **Butter**   **Eggs**   **Baking powder**

Step 3
Put the butter and sugar into a mixing bowl and cream together with a wooden spoon until fluffy. If you wish, you can use an electric mixer for steps 3, 4, and 5.

Step 4
Add the eggs to the bowl one at a time and gently beat into the mixture.

Step 5
Add the flour, baking powder, and vanilla extract and beat until thoroughly combined. The mixture should be a thick liquid. If it's stiff and won't pour, add milk a little at a time until the mixture becomes a thick liquid.

Beating with a spoon

Beating with an electric mixer

Step 6
Put half the cake batter into the second mixing bowl.

Step 7
Now add green food coloring to one bowl and red to the other. Add the gel in a tiny blob (about half the size of your pinkie fingernail) and gently mix. Keep adding color until you have the shade you want.

Baking pan

Green batter

Step 8
Use a spatula to scoop the green batter into the two cake pans, dividing it equally. Smooth the top of the batter with the spatula.

Step 9
Bake the two green layers in the center of the oven for 20 minutes. To test if the cakes are baked, insert a metal skewer into one cake. If it comes out clean, the cakes are ready. Use oven mitts to remove the pans from the oven and stand them on wire racks.

After about 10 minutes, carefully remove the cakes from the pans and place them back on the racks to cool.

Baked cake layer

Step 10
Wash and re-grease the pans and then repeat steps 8 and 9 with the red batter.

Step 11 To make the frosting, use a spoon or electric mixer to combine the sieved powdered sugar, butter, and cream cheese together until thick and smooth.

Add the white frosting color little by little, mixing well until the frosting turns white.

Sifting powdered sugar

Cream cheese

Step 12 To reveal the bright colors inside the sponge layers, trim the outer edge, or crust, from the side of each cake. Use a serrated knife to do this, carefully slicing off just a paper-thin layer of sponge.

Step 13 To assemble the cake, place a red layer on the serving plate. If the cake has risen unevenly or is slightly domed, use a serrated knife to slice off any high points and create a flat surface. Smear on a thick layer of frosting with a spatula.

Step 14 Place the green layer on top of the frosting. Keep adding the layers with frosting sandwiched between them.

Step 15 Once the fourth layer (green) is in place, smear a layer of frosting on top of the cake and top off with sprinkles and your choice of decorations.

Merry Christmas!

Glossary

beat

To blend a mixture of ingredients until they are smooth with equipment such as a spoon, fork, hand whisk, or electric mixer.

cream together

To beat butter or margarine, usually with sugar, to make it light and fluffy.

drizzle

To trickle a thin stream of liquid (such as runny frosting or a sauce) over food.

edible

Something that can be eaten.

knead

To press, squeeze, and fold dough with your hands to make it smooth and stretchy.

preheat

To turn on an oven so it is at the correct temperature for cooking a particular dish before the food is placed inside.

rub in

To use the fingers to rub flour (or other dry ingredients) into a fat, such as butter. This technique creates a breadcrumb-like mixture that is used to make pastry, crumbles, or scones.

simmer

To heat gently, staying just below a boiling temperature.

templates

Shaped pieces of a material such as cardboard that are used as a pattern for cutting out.

traditional

Something that has been a custom, belief, or practice for a long time and has been passed on from one generation to the next.

Index

Further Information

Steele, Victoria. *101 Quick & Easy Cupcake and Muffin Recipes.*
CreateSpace Independent Publishing Platform, 2014.

Learn more about Christmas here!
https://www.dkfindout.com/us/more-find-out/festivals-and-holidays/
christmas/